Goa Travel Guide

Sightseeing, Hotel, Restaurant & Shopping Highlights

Gary Jennings

Copyright © 2014, Astute Press
All Rights Reserved.

No part of this publication may be reproduced, stored in a retrieval system, or transmitted, in any form or by any means without the prior written permission of the publisher, nor be otherwise circulated in any form of binding or cover other than that in which it is published and without similar condition being imposed on the subsequent purchaser.

If there are any errors or omissions in copyright acknowledgements the publisher will be pleased to insert the appropriate acknowledgement in any subsequent printing of this publication.

Although we have taken all reasonable care in researching this book we make no warranty about the accuracy or completeness of its content and disclaim all liability arising from its use

Table of Contents

Goa **6**
    Culture 8
    Location & Orientation 8
    Climate & When to Visit 9

Sightseeing Highlights **10**
    Spice Plantations in Savoi 10
    Dudh Sagar Falls 11
    Cruises 11
    Cotigao Wildlife Sanctuary 12
    Ancestral Museum (Big Foot) 13
    Abyss Marine Aquarium 13
    Chapoli Dam 14
    Ashvek Vintage Car World Museum 15
    Fort Aguada 15
    Kuskem Waterfall & Cotigao Wildlife Sanctuary 16
    Arvalem Caves 17
    Goa State Museum 17
    Nanus Fort 18
    Splashdown Water Park 18
    Wax World Museum 19
    Beaches 20
        Anjuna Beach & Flea Market 20
        Arambol Beach 20
        Baga & Calangute Beaches 21
        Candolim Beach 21
        Benaulim Beach 21
        Chapora & Vagator Beaches 22
        Colva Beach 22
        Mandrem, Morjim & Asvem Beaches 22
        Pololem Beach 23
        Patnem Beach 23
        Cavelossim, Morbor & Varca Beaches 23
    Casinos **23**
        Casino Royale 24
        Casino Carnival 24
        Casino Caravela 25

Anjunem Dam 25
Activities 26
   Snorkeling & Scuba Diving 26
   Water Sports 27
   Fishing 27
   Crocodile & Dolphin Sightseeing 27
   Camping & Trekking 28
   Go-Karting 28

Recommendations for the Budget Traveller 29
  Places To Stay 29
   Estrela Do Mar 29
   Valentine's Retreat 30
   Royal Park Beach Resort 30
   Prainha Resort by the Sea 31
   Ondas Do Mar Beach Resort 31
  Places to Eat & Drink 32
   A Reverie 32
   Baba Au Rhum 33
   Tito's Multi-Cuisine 34
   Café La Musica 34
   German Bakery 35
  Places to Shop 36
   Anjuna Market 36
   Calangute Market Square 36
   Mapusa Friday Market 37
   Baga Saturday Market 38

Goa

Goa is the smallest state in India and visitors come from far and wide to enjoy its idyllic beaches and sunshine. Goa offers colonial architecture, luxurious coastal resorts, bustling markets and its party atmosphere is legendary. Goa is situated on the west coast of India and is easily reachable from Mumbai, one of India's major air gateways.

Goans are friendly and visitors are typically welcomed with colorful saris and gleaming smiles in the moist shades of the green tropical foliage. Goa was ruled for centuries by colonial powers and the evidence of the British and Portuguese rule has resulted in a fusion of West and East. This has created beautiful examples of architecture and a dynamic culture represented in the lively festivals and in the artistic grandeur.

Goa's churches and centuries-old fortifications were inspired by the Portuguese and the area offers good sightseeing opportunities. Authentic handicrafts (bamboo and shell work), cashews and spicy seafood can be found on every corner. Goa is also one of the few states in India where you can buy alcohol readily. One of the best ways to explore Goa is to hire a scooter or a motorbike and explore it at your own leisure.

Goa has a well-developed tourist infrastructure and English is widely spoken. If you want to avoid India's downsides you can easily do that here with Goa's slow pace of life and many spotless restaurants. There is always something interesting going on, whether it is a trance party on the beach or an active street market.

Goa has been a popular travel destination since the 1960's and is also a favorite with the alternative crowd as it is popular with New Age travelers and its appeal draws widely. They enjoy the laid-back vibe and inexpensive lodging while others enjoy the packaged holidays and the five-star accommodations or nice guesthouses at economical prices for those on a budget. Goa's resorts, hotels and other tourist businesses have flourished in recent years all along the northern coast.

Culture

Goa has a relaxed, easygoing culture and has a mix of people of different religions who coexist in harmony and peace. Goa has been described as 'The Rome of the Orient' as it was a former European territory for almost 450 years. Over the last few decades, Goa has become the most happening holiday destination in India and it is the most westernized state of India. You will find some Goans of a bohemian persuasion as they enjoy the 'tropical lifestyle' which includes the 'siesta' from 1pm to 4 pm during the hottest part of the day. Goa caters to as many travelers each year as to its own population. Some of the beaches are quiet and perfect for a peaceful, relaxing day. Other beaches are more lively with trendy kiosks, watersports, beachside restaurants, flea markets and nightclubs. You can also find moonlit parties and river cruises here.

Many Goans are passionate about dance, music, food and drama and they love their beaches, churches, monuments, temples and birdwatching. Goa's rich biodiversity was recently compared to that of Congo and the Amazon Basin of Brazil by the National Geographic magazine.

Location & Orientation

Goa is well connected by air to all the main cities in India. The Dabolim airport is located 19 miles from the city capital of Panaji. The airport is owned by the Indian Navy and has many chartered flights from the UK and other European countries. The national airline of India, Air India also operates international flights to Goa.

Goa is also connected to many cities of India through railways. Vasco-da-Gama and Margoa are the two main railway stations, both in the south of Goa. Traveling on the Konkan railway offers beautiful views en route.

Goa is connected to Belgaum, Pune, Mangalore, Mumbai, Hubli, Bangalore and elsewhere by buses that operate at regular intervals. The bus service is usually operated from the huge Kadamba bus stand in Panaji.

Climate & When to Visit

It is advisable to avoid Goa during its monsoon season (November-February) when it rains heavily making transportation sometimes problematic. During the monsoons, Goa receives an average annual rainfall of 2600 – 3500 mm. It is not safe to visit the beaches during the monsoons as the sea turns violent and the sand becomes soaked. The peak season in Goa is from October to March and you can experience Goa at its best during this time. After the monsoons the Goa weather becomes more pleasant, seas become calm and placid and the skies clear up. Every building and monument looks like it has been washed clean. The summers are a little harsh with the maximum temperature reaching 34° Celsius. Winters, on the other hand, can hardly be called winters as the minimum temperature never drops below 17° Celsius.

Sightseeing Highlights

Spice Plantations in Savoi

H No A 14, Near Betar Temple
Arla Bazar, Keri, Ponda, Goa - 403401
Tel: +91 9326130087/+91 8322340039
http://www.tropicalspiceplantation.com/

The spice plantation in Savoi covers an area of more than 100 acres and is more than 200 years old. It is 25 miles from Panjim, located in the village of Savoi. There is a pond situated inside the plantation that attracts lots of birds of different varieties like koel, cuckoos, owls, cousals, maina, pitas, horn bills, large eagles, parrots and many more.

An experienced guide will describe the characteristics of the spices, plants and their medicinal properties. Nutmeg, black pepper, cardamom, vanilla, cloves, cinnamon, chilies, betel nut palm and coriander are a few spices that can be found at this plantation. Tropical fruits like custard apples, bananas, papaya, citrus fruits and pineapples are also grown here.

Dudh Sagar Falls

Near Mollem Police Check Post
Collem, Goa - 403410
Tel: +91 9766337105

The Dudh Sagar Falls are situated on the peaks of the Western Ghats and offer amazing scenery and unrivalled beauty. The water falls from a height of 603 meters in streams down the mountainside. Dudh Sagar means ocean of milk and this is one of Goa's most attractive picnic spots. The falls culminate in gushing cascades. Get your camera ready!

Cruises

Contrans, Britona, Mandovi River
Panjim, Goa - 403001
Tel: + 91 9823050196

Some private operators as well as the Goa Tourism department organize cruises on the River Mandovi. We recommend an hour-long cruise which leaves from the Santa Monica jetty.

Folk artists perform live on the jetty. For private parties these cruises can be hired on an hourly basis also.

A Dolphin Fantasy cruise gives you a chance to see the amazing creatures in their playful mood. A Pearl of The Orient cruise will show you both the cultural and natural heritage of Goa. It is a cruise-cum-walking tour in which you get a chance to visit the areas World Heritage Monuments. Alternatively the Backwater cruise lets you enjoy the mangrove forests and you can taste the Goan food on board. You can expect to pay $2 for sunset cruise, $2 for sundown cruise, $3 for full moon cruise, $5 for dolphin fantasy cruise (includes snacks), $11 for backwater thrills (includes lunch and refreshment) and $5 for the pearl of the orient.

Cotigao Wildlife Sanctuary

Wildlife Eco Tourism, Mollem
Collem, Goa - 403410
Tel: + 91 8322612211

The Cotigao Wildlife Sanctuary is Goa's second largest sanctuary and it is great for a day trip. On display are snakes, frogs, birds, monkeys and insects.

Ancestral Museum (Big Foot)

Katem, near the Church
Salcette, Loutulim, Goa - 403718
Tel: +91 8322777034

The Ancestral museum is also known as Big Foot and is privately owned by Maendra Jocelino Araujo Alvares. The museum offers an open-air display which recreates the life of rural Goa. The art gallery displays works by artists of national and statewide fame.

In the handicraft centre, Goan artifacts are sold and you can also visit the Big Foot restaurant with its dance floor. You can also see the Boca da Vaca spring, rubber plantations, a spice yard, bird habitat and more. The major highlight of the museum is the huge 14-metre statue of the great Sant Mirabai which was carved in exactly 30 days by the owner of the museum. The entry fee to the museum is minimal and it is open 365 days from 8am to 6.30pm.

Abyss Marine Aquarium

National Highway Verna

The Abyss Marine Aquarium is popular with both young and old and is an underwater reality that will take you beyond your imagination. Here you will find statues depicting traditional activities of Goan fishermen and you can see a variety of eye-catching marine fish which are kept in aquariums.

There are a mix of unique, attractive, sophisticated and harmful fishes which are kept safe in closed aquariums. You can also catch, play and view the fish in the open aquariums. Fish on display here are imported from Lakshadweep Islands, Coastal Arabian Sea, Australia, Indonesia, Japan, Pakistan and China.

Chapoli Dam

Canacona

The Chapoli Dam is located at a scenic spot that extends westward from the famous Sahyadris. The dam is situated deep down the valley between the hills and the dam is an excellent place to stop and to take a break. There are no facilities for accommodation at the dam site, though some good hotels and guesthouses can be found at Palolem Beach and in Canacona town. Chapoli Dam is surrounded by rolling hills and is blessed with great natural beauty. Fishing is also possible in the dam waters.

Ashvek Vintage Car World Museum

Panajii Madgoan highway
Nuvem, Salcete, Goa
Tel: +91 8322731312

The Ashvek Vintage Car World museum is Goa's only museum that displays more than a dozen vintage cars. These cars are sourced from Goa and from nearby areas like Belgam, Sawantwadi and Kholapur. The museum was established to spread awareness of vintage cars amongst the youth by Pradeep Naik.

The cars are preserved and also restored here. Some of the cars are in good working condition and are hired for movie filming, joy rides and weddings. The Ashvek Vintage Car World also organizes vintage car rallies in Goa. The museum is open from Monday to Saturday from 9am to 6pm.

Fort Aguada

Sinquerim, Candolim

Fort Aguada is the most impressive fort that has been preserved in Goa and is known as a landmark in Goan history. To the North side of the fort, a rampart of brown-red laterite juts into the bay which forms the jetty between two sandy coves. This is a pictorial spot known as Sinquerim Beach.

The fort can be reached by road. The Portuguese lighthouse inside the fort was made in the 1864 and is the oldest in Asia. The lighthouse looks down over the sand, sea and the palm trees of Mandovi on one side to Calangute Beach and tip of the Cubo Palace on the other.

The Taj Village is located here now and was singled out by the Taj group to attract tourism to the area. The Fort Aguada resorts and hotels are among some of the most expensive hotels in India.

Fort Aguada is well worth a visit and the views from the four-storey lighthouse are superb.

Kuskem Waterfall & Cotigao Wildlife Sanctuary

Canacona Taluka, South Goa

The Kuskem waterfall is best visited during the rainy season as its water dries up during the summers. The water falls from a lofty place giving the impression of a cascade of milky water. Kuskem waterfall is located at a distance of 12 km from Hathipal, which is an entry point to the Cotigao Wildlife Sanctuary.

It is the best place to unwind and one can stay in the eco-cottages of the forest department at the wildlife sanctuary. An ancient temple which is located nearby is also worth exploring. This waterfall is visited by many on the way to the Wildlife Sanctuary.

Arvalem Caves

Town of Sanquelim

The Arvalem Caves are small and their origin is not certain. Some believe them to be of Buddhist origin and some claim them to be of Brahmin origin. The different shafts of the carved lingas inside the cave are similar to those found at the famous Ellora and Elephanta caves. These features were designed in the Buddhist cave style; rocks are cut in to laterite stone with the viharas at the southern end and the sanctuary at the northern end.

Goa State Museum

4c/Fi-2, BSNL Building End, Edc Complex
Near Ktc Bus Stand, Patto, Panjim, Goa   403001
Tel: +91 8322438006

The Goa State Museum is open from 9am to 5pm from Monday to Friday and the museum displays various items like wooden statues of different Christian saints, copper plate writing of Kadamba Kings, bronze and stone sculpture, contemporary art, terracotta items of Indus Valley Civilization, miniatures of Mughal Paintings and a huge chariot from the Chandreshwar Temple located near Margao. This museum also displays a number of lottery machines from Portuguese times.

Nanus Fort

Satari Taluka, North Goa

Nanus Fort is a historical fort that was built by Shivaji in the seventeenth century and was taken by the Portuguese later. Today only the remains of the fort can be seen. The fort can be reached by taxi or bike and in order to get to the fort one needs to climb up a small hill. The nearest town to Nanus Fort is Valpoi.

Splashdown Water Park

Near Hotel Riviera De Goa
Anjuna, Goa - 403509
+91 9637424023
http://www.splashdowngoa.com/

Splashdown is the number one water park in Goa. The facility offers 5 pools, flumes, slides and other fun features. The Water Park has been designed in a way that people from all age groups can enjoy.

It gives you a chance to rediscover your childhood and is an excellent place to spend time with your friends and family. Come to Splashdown to celebrate an occasion, be it a family get-together or a birthday party. This is a place where a splash of fun is mixed with little adventure and it will help you to forget all your troubles – as well as your age.

Wax World Museum

Gandi Circle,
Old Goa
Goa - 403404
Tel: +91 9970126202
http://www.waxworld.in/

India's second wax museum is located in Goa and each figure is carefully made of paraffin wax. The teeth and eyes are artificial but the hair is natural.

The museum has more than 30 lifesize statues of famous personalities of Indian heritage, culture and religion. One of the major attractions is the sculpture of the 'Last Supper' - it weighs 500 kilos and is 22 feet in height.

A guide will take you through the museum and explain all about the statues, the field they represent and how and why the statue was made. The guided tour is available in Hindi and English.

The main attractions include Radha Krishna and Mahatma Gandhi. There is also a statue that called 'Say No to Drugs' which depicts the side effects of drug use. The museum has a small gift shop where candles of different shapes, designs and fragrances are available for sale.

Beaches

Here is a synopsis of what to expect from Goa's best beaches.

Agonda Beach

The isolated and long stretch of Agonda Beach is just perfect for someone looking to get away from their busy life. It is quiet and not very crowded and if you are looking for relaxation, this is the beach for you. You can enjoy the nature and stillness by renting a simple hut on the beach. You can expect to find a few souvenir stalls and restaurants.

Anjuna Beach & Flea Market

The Wednesday Flea Market at Anjuna Beach is growing every week Here you can sit in one of the shacks all day long and just listen to the psychedelic trance music. The most happening spot of Anjuna beach is Curlies, which is set at the southern side of the beach. Anjuna's popular Paradiso Disco is also situated at this side of the beach.

Arambol Beach

This beach offers lots of alternative therapies like meditation, tai-chi, reiki and yoga. Dolphin sightseeing trips and water sports are also offered. The nightlife of this beach is more relaxed and to the North of Arambol Beach is the the Tricol Fort and the deserted Keri Beach.

Baga & Calangute Beaches

Calangute Beach is the most commercial and busiest beach in Goa. It is jam packed with the foreigners tanning themselves on the sun lounges and with the Indians that come to watch them. Baga Beach starts where Calangute Beach ends and is often less crowded and better developed. A wide variety of water sports are offered here. There are many restaurants in the area that offer a good variety of booze and food. Baga is well known for its happening nightlife including the popular Café Mambo and Club Tito.

Candolim Beach

This long stretch of beach is lined with a seemingly endless number of bars and shacks and is an excellent alternative if you want to avoid the crowds of Baga and Calangute. This lively, clean and peaceful beach is located next to the Aguada Fort.

Benaulim Beach

Benaulim Beach is a laid back and beautiful beach that is known for its fishing industry. This beach is not for the party animal but offers dolphin sightseeing trips and water sports.

Chapora & Vagator Beaches

This is the center for Goa's trance parties. Vagator Beach is located under a steep cliff and is in three sections – Ozran, Big Vagator and Little Vagator. Disco valley is located nearby. The accommodation in this area is inland and not right on the beach but many people like staying here long-term.

Colva Beach

Colva Beach is one of the favorite beaches for Indian tourists and day-trippers arrive here by the bus load. The beach is especially busy in October when pilgrims come to visit the nearby Colva Church. The area offers many budget hotels, beach shacks, small restaurants, bars and food stalls.

Mandrem, Morjim & Asvem Beaches

Mandrem, Morjim and Asvem beaches are isolated and usually empty and do not offer many facilities for visitors. You can expect to find makeshift accommodations, camping facilities and just a few beach hotels. These beaches are well known for their turtle population.

Pololem Beach

This charming beach is semicircular and has soft sand and shady palm trees. There are no permanent structures here but temporary coco huts are offered, and these are constructed every year.

Patnem Beach

If you want to relax, Patnem Beach is a small beach that is made for you. It is nestled between two cliffs and gorgeous beach huts with attached bathrooms are on offer.

Cavelossim, Morbor & Varca Beaches

These pristine fishing beaches are the centerpoint of Goa's most luxurious resorts. The beaches are clean and have white sand and you will find only a few shacks, peddlers and water sport operators.

Casinos

A trip to Goa is incomplete without a visit to a casino and Goa offers some of the best casinos in India.

Casino Royale

Noah's Ark, Panjim
Tel: +91 832 651 9471
http://www.casinoroyalegoa.com/

Casino Royale is the most popular and largest floating casino in Goa. It is situated on a large boat which is anchored in the Mandovi River. It has 12000 square feet of space for gaming and has 30 slot machines, 50 gaming tables and tournaments are held every week. Packages are available and range from $50 to $90 per person, which includes alcoholic drinks, food, playing chips and variety show entertainment. The entertainment in this casino begins at 10pm. The games include American Roulette, Black Jack, Texas Holdem Poker, Baccarat, Slot Machines, Casino Wars, Money Wheel and more.

Casino Carnival

D.B. Marg, Panjim Residency, Panjim
Tel: +91 8888807256 & +91 8322222092
http://www.casinocarnival.in/

The Casino Carnival has two venues: aboard a boat on the Mandovi River and inside the Marriott Hotel, Goa next to Mirama Beach. The Casino Carnival at Marriott has the largest range of slot machines and a large variety of table games. The floating casino has 28 gaming tables and four operational decks and they offer a VIP room for high rollers.

Live entertainment is available on the gaming floor. The entry fee per person for the floating casino is $40 which includes snacks, house brand alcohol, a buffet dinner, casino entrance tax and entertainment. They offer games like Poker, Slot Machines, American Roulette and Blackjack.

Casino Caravela

Fisheries Department Building
D. B Marg, Panaji
Tel: +91 832 2433289
http://www.casinocaravela.com/

This was Goa's first offshore casino. Casino Caravala offers a VIP room, games and a restaurant that serves haute cuisine and has a modern jetty. There is live entertainment across three areas; casino floor, sundeck and the restaurant. Casino Caravala accommodates 300 guests and has 10 slot machines and more than 100 gaming positions. The entry fee is $30 per person which includes $20 worth of complimentary playing chips.

Anjunem Dam

Sanquelim-Begaum Highway
Chorla Ghat

Anjunem Dam is one of the best places to enjoy the environment and its mystic charms. The dam is located in the Sylvan Valley close to the Morlemgad Peak and below Vagheri Hill (Goa's highest peak).

For accommodation, you can stay at the rest house of the irrigation department or at a rest house of the forest department which are located above the dam. You can also stay at a private eco resort which is located in Chorla Ghat. Anjunem Dam offers an enchanting ambience and visitors often return every season.

Activities

A trip to Goa offers a great chance to try out some new watersports. Goa's beaches have temperate waters and can be enjoyed by beginners and the more experienced. Listed here are a few highlights of the water activities that you can enjoy.

Snorkeling & Scuba Diving

Goa offers some amazing scuba diving sites near to Grand Island that include Davy Jones Locker, Suzy's Wreck, Umma Gumma Reef, Bounty Bay and Shelter Cove. The best months for snorkeling are from October to April when you can see some mesmerizing marine life. Snorkeling trips cost from $25.

Water Sports

You can choose from jetskiing, parasailing, waterskiing, kitesurfing, catamaran sailing, banana rides and wakeboarding. Prices vary for these activities but you can expect to pay $20 for jetskiing, $15 to 35 for parasailing, $6-10 for a banana ride, $35 for wakeboarding and kitesurfing, $20 for windsurfing and $30 for waterskiing. Atlantis Water Sports are the biggest operators on Calangute Beach.

Fishing

From October to December, the best time for fishing is late afternoon and early morning. Boat tours for fishing are run from Condolim Beach at an average cost of $20. This trip includes all day fishing or deepsea fishing expeditions.

Crocodile & Dolphin Sightseeing

One of the most popular activities in Goa is Crocodile and Dolphin spotting and the best time for such trips is November to May. You can expect to pay $20 for Dolphin trips and $25 for Crocodile trips.

Camping & Trekking

The best time to go trekking is from October to December and the best places to hike and trek include Devils Canyon, Sahyadri Hills, The Chandrasurya Temple, Mollem Wildlife Sanctuary and Castle rock to Kuveshi Falls.

Go-Karting

The latest craze in Goa is go-karting. The 1/5-mile go-karting track at Arpora is located near to the Indigo Night Market. The cost is $3.50 for 10 laps.

Recommendations for the Budget Traveller

Places to Stay

Estrela Do Mar

Khobra Vaddo, Baga Calangute, Bardez, Goa 403516
Tel: +91 9011018191 / +91 832 2279085
http://www.estreladomargoa.net/

Estrela Do Mar is located right on Calangute Beach and offers all the facilities of a resort with its 82 beautifully designed rooms, garden restaurant, swimming pool and open air rooftop restaurant. The resort also offers Jain food for vegetarians. Accommodation begins at $80 for a single room.

Valentine's Retreat

Sequeira Waddo, Candolim
Bardez, Goa 403515
Tel: +91 0832 2479828 / 2479431
http://www.valentinesretreat.com/index.htm

Valentine's Retreat is on the Calangute-Condolim beach stretch. The resort offers 27 rooms with balconies and the restaurant serves delicious Indian, Continental, Chinese and local cuisine. Guests can visit the bar which offers a range of imported as well as Indian spirits. They are also well stocked with cocktails. Valentine's Retreat offers facilities including pickup and dropoff at the railway station, bus stop or airport on request. Accommodation is priced between $80 and $120 per night.

Royal Park Beach Resort

1/230-A, Holiday St., Gaurawado
Calangute, Bardez, Goa
Tel: 91-832-2279111, 9822475888, 9921276999
http://royalparkbeachresort.net/

Royal Park Beach Resort is a luxurious Spa beach resort at Calangute Beach which offers 5 star facilities.

The suites and rooms are elegant and a honeymoon suite is available. The other facilities offered by the resort include a Jacuzzi, swimming pool, health centre, complimentary Wi-Fi, indoor games, gift shop, multi-cuisine restaurant and a coffee shop. Accommodation varies between $90 and $130 per night.

Prainha Resort by the Sea

Dona Paula, Goa 403004
Tel: (0832) 2453881/2/3, 6453892
http://www.prainha.com/home.html

Prainha Resort is delightfully surrounded by palm trees and tropical vegetation. There are 44 cottage style rooms and features in-house eateries including Harbor Lights, a bar that serves a choice of cocktails as well as The Palm Grove which is a bar/restaurant. Tourist sites, the airport and the railway station are close by. Accommodation begins at $100.

Ondas Do Mar Beach Resort

Holiday Street, Gauravaddo, Calangute, Bardez, Goa, India 403516
Tel: +91-832-2277526 / +91-7798657775
http://www.ondasdomargoa.com/index.htm

The Ondas Do Mar Beach Resort is located nearby Calangute Beach and has 30 air-conditioned rooms beautifully designed in a Portuguese-style with balconies.

They have a multi-cuisine restaurant that serves guests a choice of Chinese, Indian and Continental cuisine. Their outdoor pool is decorated with sunloungers. One can take a stroll or lounge in the calm ambience of their garden space. There is also an in-house massage center. The accommodation starts at $80.

Places to Eat & Drink

A Reverie

Holiday - Street, Calangute
Goa, India
Phone: +91-9823174927/+91-9823505550
http://www.whatsupgoa.com/areverie

A Reverie, located on the holiday street of Calangute, is the place for modern European food. The food is served in innovative ways, influenced by different cuisines from around the world. Crystal chandeliers and disco balls present soft lighting. They are open for dinner (only) from 7.00pm and in-house specialties of include teriyaki boneless chicken, tropical dessert platter, wasabi prawns, prawn l lobster. The average cost of a meal for 2 people is $40 to $80.

Baba Au Rhum

French Cafe, Bakery & Pizzeria
House No 453
Cuddos Waddo, Arpora
Bardez, Goa 403518
(Located in Arpora, on the way to Baga after the Saturday Night Market.)
Tel: +91 9822078759/+91 9657210468
http://www.whatsupgoa.com/GoaRestaurants/index.php?etabid=69

Baba Au Rhum is a delightful café in a calm residential area just off the main road to Anjuna. They have a delicious menu of sandwiches, hearty salads, fruit juices, pastries and baked delicacies. Baba Au Rhum is the most popular restaurant on the north side of Goa and you can spend a relaxed afternoon here. Baba Au Rhum is separated into a pizzeria where tourists convene for a good laugh while enjoying good food and a bakery that is a supplier to hotels and restaurants across North Goa.

Baba Au Rhum prepare their sandwiches with breads that are fresh and baked on their own premises and their delectable pizza is fired fresh in their wooden oven. The pastry specialties to look for are strawberry tart, mille feuilles, lemon tart and chocolate éclair. Meals are priced between $6 and $16. Baba Au Rhum is is closed on Wednesday's.

Tito's Multi-Cuisine

Tito's Lane,
Saunta Vaddo, Baga Calangute,
Bardez, Goa 403517
Tel: +919822765002
http://www.whatsupgoa.com/GoaRestaurants/index.php?etabid=80

Tito's is an uncovered multi-cuisine restaurant that offers local, oriental and continental dishes. The bar serves both international and Indian spirits, with vintage wines from around the globe. Tito's Courtyard plays a host to international and local entertainment. Their specialty is the wicked waffle, freshly baked, yummy French style crepes and Belgium waffles accompanied with tropical and seasonal fruits and Belgian chocolate. Their Sushi bar is a must try as it offers an assortment of fish prepared as Sashimi and Nigiri. The average meal for 2 costs $30 to $70.

Café La Musica

Beach Shacks
Baga Beach (down Tito's lane), Baga, Goa 403516
Tel: +919923447137
http://www.whatsupgoa.com/GoaRestaurants/index.php?etabid=324

Café La Musica is a beachside lounge on Baga Beach. It offers an exotic menu that features oriental food together with delightful cocktails and a well stocked bar.

The ambience of this beach shack is stylish and laid back and it is open throughout the year. Café La Musica frequently hosts fabulous beachside parties. The menu offers South East Asian food and delicacies like Malaysian Penang Curry, Vietnamese pho, Nasi Goreng, pla rad prik and fresh Sushi. Their menu also includes an all day breakfast. The dishes cost from $6 to $15.

German Bakery

Vegetarian & Organic
Market Road,
403509, Anjuna, Goa
Tel: +919096058775
http://www.whatsupgoa.com/GoaRestaurants/index.php?etabid=172

German Bakery is a bakery and food café in South Anjuna. With great music, comfortable booths, complimentary Wi-Fi internet access and healthy food, this is a place where an afternoon is comfortably spent. The menu has everything from herbal teas, wheatgrass, fresh tofu, espresso coffees, salads, hummus and pizza. Their sandwiches are made from their in-house bread. This popular raw, healthy and vegetarian food café is located in a large garden property.

German Bakery is famous for its natural and healthy food products like organic honey, homemade preserves, vinegar, fresh yak cheese and apricot oil. Their menu offers a choice of milkshakes, lassi, smoothies, fresh fruit juices and a blend of energy providing juices including coconut juice, carrot cleanser, aloe vera and many more. A highlight of the German Bakery is their homemade ice creams.

Places to Shop

Anjuna Market

Anjuna Beach, Anjuna, Bardez, India
Every Wednesday – 8am to 12pm

The famous Anjuna market is also known as the flea market. It is held in the midst of coconut palms every Wednesday morning between the fallow rice paddies and the rocky beach of Anjuna. The market is a world of crowds, color, talking and clamor and all types of goods from ornamental crafts, spices, local Goanese goods, Tibetan and Kashmiri handicrafts, jewelry, Goan trance music, fabrics and clothing. The market offers an assortment of goods but, as in many shops in Goa, be sure to bargain.

Calangute Market Square

Calangute Beach
Everyday – 8am to 8pm

Calangute Beach is nine miles north of Panaji, the Goan Capital. The beach is covered with beautiful palm trees and stretches about four miles. The streets are packed with shops that offer an extensive range of goods including souvenirs, leather items, metal crafts, jewelry and clothes, not just from Goa but also from other parts of India.

The entire beach stretch is full of hawkers selling sarongs, shacks, fortune-tellers and astrologers waiting to predict the fortune of tourists. Calangute also offers a Tibetan market and Kashmiri merchants come to Goa with their embroidery, carpets and other products.

Mapusa Friday Market

Near Mapusa Municipal Market, Mapusa
Every Friday – 8am to 6.30pm

Mapusa Market takes place every Friday and this is where Goan customers like to buy foodstuffs. The Mapusa Market offers a wide range of locally produced vegetables, fresh fish and interesting fruits from mangoes and plantain bananas to jackfruit. Spices, preserves and pickles, earthen pots, channa baskets coir mats, glass bangles, prawns and dried fish, junk jewelry, clothing, the very famous country liquor and Goan 'chouricos' are sold here at very reasonable prices.

Baga Saturday Market

Baga Beach Area, Baga
Every Saturday – 8am to 12pm

Baga Saturday Market is somewhat similar to the Anjuna Flea Market. Baga Beach has many beach huts and shacks that sell thirst-quenching Feni and scrumptious Goan food. The dynamic Saturday market is lit up with lamps so it looks beautiful under the night sky. The stalls sell clothes, bric-à-brac, trinkets, Goanese cuisine and other exotic delicacies. There are also lots of handicraft shops where wood carvings, palmistry, tarot reading and funky haircuts are also offered. Additionally, live bands create a carnival like atmosphere which makes the place "rock"!

Printed in Great Britain
by Amazon